Happy 58th
Ribby,
Chloe, & Klibi
& Beth

i'm just a cat mattress...

Illustrations by Susan Sturgill

I'M JUST A CAT MATTRESS
Copyright © 2006 Crescent Hill Books and Susan Sturgill

This book may be purchased for fund-raising purposes or sales promotional use. For information, please contact Crescent Hill Books, 2410 Frankfort Avenue, Louisville, KY 40206.

First Edition

ISBN 10: 1-889937-10-X
ISBN 13: 978-1-889937-10-6

Library of Congress Cataloguing-in-Publication Data
CIP data has been applied for.

Book design: Chad DeBoard and Toni Johnson
Photography: Gary Heinonen

Printed in China by Everbest Printing Company

This Book Belongs to:

_____

and I hereby grant myself permission to use and enjoy this book in the manner in which it was intended. I am permitted to freely remove these illustrations, as I understand that art this fun need not remain locked inside the pages of a book. It should be shared, displayed and enjoyed again and again.

introduction

People often ask me
where I get my ideas.

they just come to me.

★ Susan ★

I don't know...

Cats remind us that each season

has it's own sweet joy.

Seasons of the Cat

The real reason I can't stick to my diet
is because my cats hate to eat alone.

★ *Susan Sturgill* ★

Refrigerator Magnets

Our perfect companions never have fewer than four feet.

★ *Colette* ★

Movie Night

A well-known cat mantra is:

"Always Stretch Upon Waking..."

Yoga Cats

Her function is to sit and be admired.

★ *Georgina Strickland Gates* ★

That's why they call it a flower bed

The cat is the only animal
which accepts the comforts
but rejects the bondage of domesticity.

★ *Georges Louis Leclerc de Buffon* ★

Cats like to stay on top of current events

If you didn't have a cat to wake you up in the middle of the night, how would you know how much you had enjoyed sleeping?

★ *Susan Sturgill* ★

What time do you start serving breakfast?

Life is all about finding
fun in the simple things...

Boxes, Bags and Baskets

"For me, one of the pleasures of cats' company is their devotion to bodily comfort."

★ *Sir Compton Macken* ★

Couch Potatoes

Most beds sleep up to six cats.

Ten cats without the owner.

★ *Stephen Baker* ★

I'm Just a Cat Mattress

Cats like doors left open,

in case they change their minds.

★ Rosemary Nisbet ★

Cats hate closed doors

All cats enjoy the occasional evening of
mindless entertainment,
but they prefer the
educational nature programming.

★ *Susan Sturgill* ★

Cat TV

"A cat doesn't know what it wants and wants more of it."

★ *Richard Hexem* ★

Cats Like to Help

It's very hard to be polite if you're a cat.

Where does it come from? Where does it go?

The purity of a person's heart can be quickly measured by how they regard animals.

They can stare for hours

You can't own a cat.

The best you can do is be partners.

★ *Sir Harry Swanson* ★

Cats are receptive to new technology

I love cats because I enjoy my home;
and little by little,
they become its visible soul.

★ *Jean Cocteau* ★

The morning grooming ritual

"The way to keep a cat is to try to chase it away."

★ *E.W. Howe* ★

Cats like to make houseguests feel welcome

A cat improves the garden wall in sunshine,
the hearth in foul weather.

★ Judith Merkle Riley ★

Garden Ornaments

The cat is above all things, a dramatist.

★ *Margaret Benson* ★

Cats Just Want to Have Fun

To bathe a cat takes brute force,

perseverance,

courage of conviction -

and a cat.

The last ingredient is usually hardest to come by.

★ *Stephen Baker* ★

Cats do not understand the appeal of full immersion bathing

"The last thing I would accuse a cat of

is innocence."

★ *Edward Paley* ★

The Gang of Seven

There are two means of refuge from the miseries of life:

music and cats.

★ *Albert Schweitzer* ★

A cat makes coming home something to look forward to.

Bon Voyage

Animals are such agreeable friends -
they ask no questions,
they pass no criticisms.

★ *George Eliot* ★

Cats vs. Dogs

The Pet Question...

cat affection

dog affection

cat play

dog play

cat noise

mew

cat mess

dog noise

dog mess

In Kitty Heaven, the clouds are made of clean laundry and the refrigerator never closes...

★ *Susan Sturgill* ★

Kitty Heaven

No Heaven will ever Heaven be,
unless my cats are there to welcome me.

The Kitty Angel

EXPENSIVE PRESCRIPTION CHOW